I Speak in Cursive

I Speak in
in
Cursive

*A Compilation of
Poetic Words*

Quortni Fambro

I Speak in Cursive
Copyright ©2021 by Quortni Fambro

All rights reserved. Except for brief quotations in books and critical reviews, and except as permitted under the copyright laws of the United States of America, no part of this publication may be reproduced, distributed, or transmitted in any form or by any means, or stored in adatabase or retrieval system, without the prior written permission of the publisher.

ISBN-13: 978-1-7369956-0-0

Cover Artist: Sarah Katreen Hoggatt
Illustrated by ClaraLee Esther

10 9 8 7 6 5 4 3 2 1

Printed and bound in the United States of America

Acknowledgements: I would like to give a huge thanks to the women of Fort Leonard Wood's Echo 3-10 Class of 2020 for being my first audience. They gave me constructive feedback, suggestions, and took the time to listen to my work. Most importantly, they were supportive and encouraging. Thank you all! I am also thankful for the positive confinement I received during my military training, illuminating my light to focus and shine.

Contents

Introduction   vii

love

secretly enamored of you   3
struggle love   4
unreadable you   6
erotic rapture   9
feed me   11
reciprocity   12
buried needs   13
the beauty of a man   14
clung to you   16

military

to love a soldier   19
i ruck   20
navigation   22
ocs   24

nature

night gazer   27
the beauty of sight   29

emotions & sentimentals

missouri blues   33
maternal   34
a sibling's oath   35

motivational
in professional terms   41
graduation day   43
fury   44
inspiration   46
authority   48
inquisition   49

mental health & mindfulness
an idle mind's despair   53
a reflective freefall   54

uncategorical
directionless   59
be realistic   60
unsettled   61
the color black   63
90's baby   64
colors   67
as quiet as it's kept   68
an ode to jill   71
support that business   72
hormonal oblivion   74
perspective   75

Introduction

I HAVE ALWAYS BEEN INTO THE beauty of poetry. I think the stories poets can tell are a pure talent that many can relate to personally or just genuine mental entertainment for the masses. I've written several poems throughout my life, from adolescence to adulthood, but only recently was I inspired to publish some of my work. I joined the U.S. Army and had plenty of time to write in my downtime in basic training at Fort Leonard Wood in Missouri. Confinement and focus allowed me to write some of my best work yet. My creative energy was overflowing! I had so many ideas that my thoughts literally spilled onto whatever I could write on; a toilet roll in the field while in training, a pocket pad while maneuvering through the woods, or anything else I could get my hands on. My mission was to get it written down before I forgot it. It was a challenge putting this project together while in the process of becoming a Soldier. Still, I don't think it would have been as incredible had I done it any other way. I hope you all (the readers) enjoy my words. I put a ton of thought and effort into my poems. Each one was written randomly but intentionally. I hope to reintroduce classic poetry that tells the stories of life one line at a time. Give your mind a treat, and turn the pages of my first published masterpiece, *I Speak in Cursive: A Compilation of Poetic Words*.

love

secretly enamored of you

i see you from afar, and love the way that you walk;
your whole aura so masculine, i really wish we could talk.

your vibe is such a mystery, due to obvious circumstances;
i'm really plotting on how i should move,
deciding whether or not to take my chances.

i don't fear rejection, but i would love for you to say yes;
to the idea of me and you, no stress, that's god blessed.

maybe i'll follow through
and ensure this message reaches you;
and who knows that one gesture may lead to "i do".

well, maybe a bit too soon, but a woman can dream;
about a handsome man, a family, sacred vows, a union,
one team.

courage, timing, tact, professionalism, and reserve;
all reasons why i may halt, placing my feelings to the curb.

the ward of my church, i hope you caught that reference;
because i see you, i want you, you're my top tier preference.

carry on fly fellow, until we meet again.
the message is out, i didn't forget to press send.

struggle love

so focused on you, i can't see things clearly.
you bring me happiness, but it quickly becomes dreary.
i don't understand my hesitancy,
but i know something is not right.
i've always had a discerning spirit, but for some reason,
for you, against it i fight.

i should be all smiles, but in silence i cry.
because this person is not me, i'm miserable, living a lie.
you promised to avoid the same mistakes
that you made in the past;
but i guess after relations, that sentiment doesn't last.

i held on because i thought our relationship
was at the level of master.
but that was a farse, a sham, a blazing, fiery disaster.
i chose you over me, and that will never happen again;
i've declared it unbecoming, and labeled it a personal sin.

i will never fall so hard to the point i ignore my senses;
because that low is agonizing,
and it's hard climbing outta' trenches.
i love me more; this i now know.
i've regained my strength, and a healthy, radiant glow.

unreadable you

always the girl next door,
never the one he pursues.
already been through the headaches,
already paid my dues.

i catch your glances at me,
not sure what your eye contact means.
could it be disgust or interest?
things aren't always as they seem.

maybe i'm doing too much,
it's tiring figuring out.
i wanna make it be real,
cause' my love life's in a drought.

that's not to mean that i'm desperate,
that's surely never the case.
but whether you admit it or not,
there's feelings in our shared space.

stop playing with my emotions,
no need to play with my mind.
anything you want to tell me;
believe me i surely have time.

your body language confusing,
it's sort of open and shut;
don't do me like that please,
cause' i'll get stuck in a rut.

i wonder should i step up,
or let the man do his part;
but maybe it is just me,
i could be wrong from the start.

i'll let this game play out,
and rate your game of chess.
but after while i must move on,
and lay desires to rest.

soon as i make up my mind,
decide it's time to move on;
i take my cellular out,
it's your number across my phone.

erotic rapture

no silence, all sound,
room full of sensuality
no weave, no make-up,
no artificiality

i want you to see all of me,
open up those brown eyes
even before undressing me,
i see them looking over my thighs

you seem surprised by my build,
my feminine muscles glisten and glow
they do more than just look good;
i guarantee you it's not just for show

i feel the heat from your body
as you stand next to me
the sooner you get undressed,
the sooner we get to ecstasy

feel free to touch, caress,
finesse, and explore
the shyness should have left you
once you entered the door

no need to rush through the process,
i'm all for methodic
as long as your moves are all yours,
don't bring the practiced robotics

i hear your breathing, you seem excited,
don't explode just yet
you'll need that energy,
and possibly electrolytes when you break out in sweats

i'm not the dirty talker,
i like to show you all my intentions;
i heard that actions are better than words,
i bet it keeps your attention

a bare soul, so open,
and the mood so intense
the whole experience so new,
my mind is left in suspense

don't want to stop but i must,
cause' anatomy is a beast
let's both recuperate and sleep,
after we finish this feast

i need to feel your presence near
as i enter this rest;
i must admit you came to play,
possibly rated the best

feed me

feed me wisdom, feed me knowledge.
there's so much more to be learned outside of college.

feed me positivity, feed me energy.
my goals and aspirations reign high, supremacy.

feed me honesty, feed me truths.
don't lose your integrity, or be uncouth.

feed me the energy, that i feed to you.
because even the best of us need encouragement too.

feed me life, because we all must live,
and in that time, don't forget to give.

feed me happiness, because i love to smile.
those nice bright teeth add more to your style.

feed me your life stories, so i can learn about you.
i'm a judgement free space, and listen is what i will do.

feed me companionship, feed me trust,
because loyalty will always be better than lust.

feed me your inner self, feed me your soul.
that privilege is the pinnacle, almost like i struck gold.

feed me your gray hairs, and that circle band on your hand.
let's raise some grand kids, and take walks in the sand.

feed me a selfless journey, because i will be here to serve.
i'll treat you like the king you are,
and give you what you deserve.

reciprocity

provide me all the things
i make happen for you.
don't ask me for anything
that you aren't willing to do.

equality is for friendships,
bonds, and relationships too.
leave the attitude and bad habits,
and show me a side of you that's new.

i get pleasure from acts of service
and watching you thrive.
however, without reciprocation it's hard
for feelings of trust and appreciation to derive.

i don't need you to hand me the world
on a fancy gold-plated platter.
i just need you to do everything in your power
to show me, to you, i matter.

buried needs

companionship is something you can go
a lifetime and never find.
those odds are petrifying,
constantly boggling my mind.

i have so much to share,
i look forward to unraveling this gift.
i want a kindred spirit,
someone who disowns relationship rifts.

that friendship to be,
is yet to be discovered.
open up a little,
let your interesting side be uncovered.

even introverts need
that designated lifeline.
we're social creatures,
we'll need each other until the end of time.

they say a man who finds a wife,
finds a good thing.
ensure she's really the one for you,
and not fixated on the ring.

as a woman i need things
i can't always describe.
i need a mate whose patient,
cause' instructions don't always come inscribed.

my visions are sometimes deeper
than words can express.
but i hope you feel the depth of my existence
through my writing's redress.

the beauty of a man

the beauty of a man's face, the strength in his profile.
every time he strides by me, my loins run wild.

the beauty of a man's hands, so firm and strong.
when i'm in his presence, how could it ever be wrong?

the beauty of a man's back, so chiseled and defined.
his exterior so godly, both tough and refined.

the beauty of a man's arms, veins flowing full of testosterone.
everything about him magnificent, from his brain to his bones.

the beauty of a man's decision to choose his wife.
i'd guard that position, and cherish it for life.

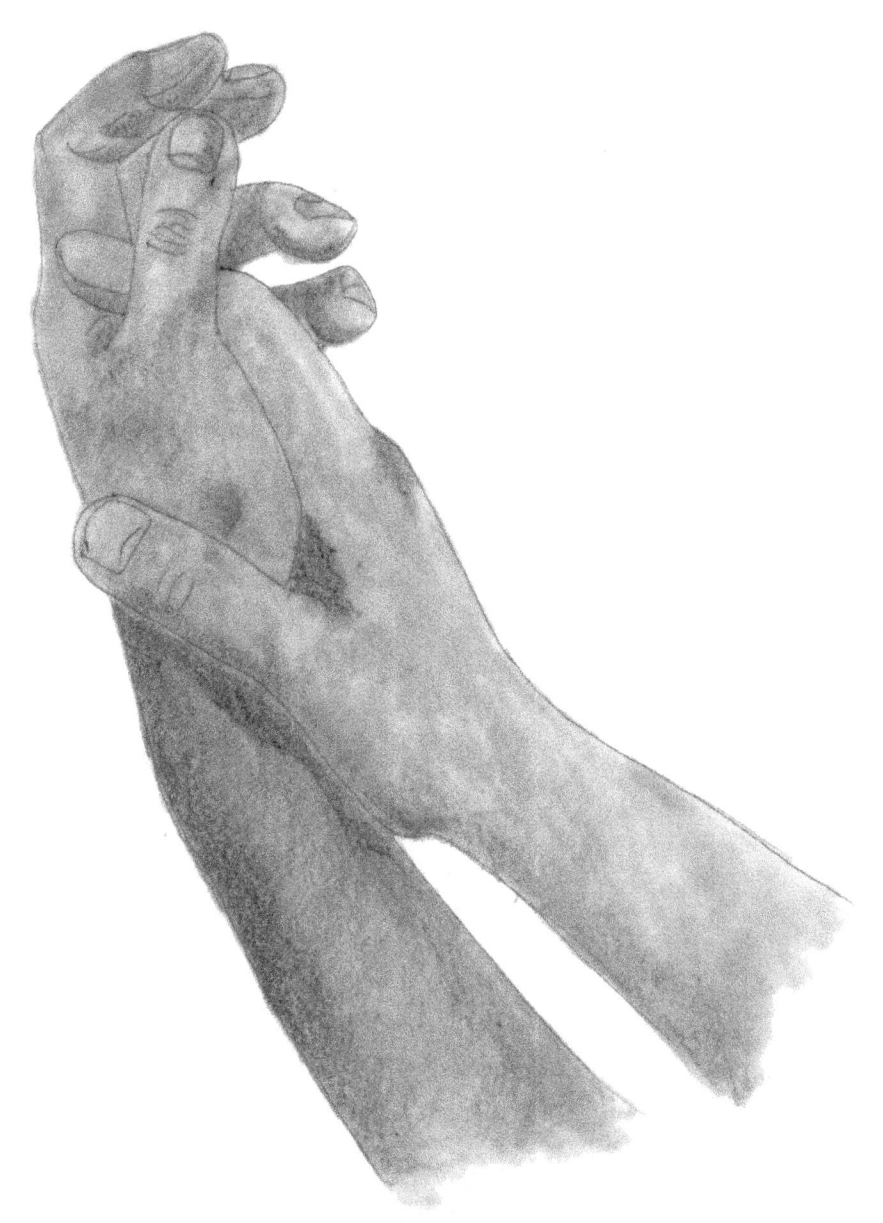

clung to you

i'm clingy, so enjoy my desire
to be in your vicinity.
just looking at your face
is god's granted serenity.

i'm clingy, but i need to be
appreciated and cherished.
don't take my being drawn to you as a weakness,
because it can all perish.

i'm clingy, but it's all in
admiration and respect.
don't insult my willingness to accept your flaws,
and mismanage the context.

i'm clingy, but do understand
this privilege can be withdrawn.
i'm into you, but i'm not a fool;
i'm not ashamed to uproot and be gone.

i'm clingy, so know that my lovin'
is genuine and pure.
in your darkest times i'll be
your medicinal and psychological cure.

i'm clingy, just be ready
to live a good life and stay.
i'm adamant about you, i give a thanks
to the most high for you when i pray.

military

to love a soldier

people change and so do
their minds.
i see the possibility in you,
but the odds aren't kind.

we're both service workers
and always on the go.
i'm tired of leaving love behind,
but obligations force me to forgo.

that one special person,
but we're both on guard.
we can't fully commit to one another,
because this lifestyle is simply hard.

you have to fully commit yourself
and focus on the mission.
it almost makes you believe in clichés
and bogus superstitions.

you have to be able to have less of heart,
because it keeps you focused on survival.
i'd rather dismiss the memory of you,
than have you as my rival.

if you believe we're meant to be,
then allow the silence to marinate.
they say that silence makes the heart grow fonder,
so this i must reiterate.

i'll return to you soon with hope and a smile,
so be ready to embrace me in the flesh.
i've held on to the memory of you from days to months,
our spirits are set to mesh.

i ruck*

i ruck for the skill, i ruck for the fight.
i pray one day it keeps me alive in the night.

i ruck in the early morning, and into the day.
hopefully that long walk leads me out of harm's way.

i ruck because i have to, sworn to it like the soldier's creed.
i've vowed to face war, both boots in the lead.

i ruck with confidence, soldiers show no fear.
because only cowards flee action, but return home accepting cheer.

i ruck with my battle buddies, we're something like a fraternity.
we go left foot, right foot, marching on into eternity.

i ruck in hopes, to rid the world of political strife;
once a soldier, always a soldier, i'll be a soldier for life.

---

* Ruck- walking or marching on various terrain from one location to another in a military manner, with a backpack (ruck sac) loaded with necessary miscellaneous items, weighing 50+ lbs., and worn for several miles at a time. Essentially, rucking is how military members haul their equipment on foot from place to place; for example, equipment can include anything from wet weather gear to toiletries.

navigation

i travel through smut, true grit, and grime.
i navigate terrain and monitor time.

i travel through rain, and sleet, and snow.
i navigate through it all, i'm ready to go.

i travel through lands to complete the mission.
we navigate anywhere we have suspicions.

i travel through politics and presidential speeches.
we navigate anywhere our m4 reaches.

i travel through my mind and analyze my decision.
i navigate the woods and hold my position.

i travel through opinions and social barriers.
i navigate disease and the foreign carriers.

i travel through the world in my army greens.
i navigate situations with my battle teams.

i travel to our wars, that's the life i chose.
i navigate to live; in war anything goes.

ocs

don't compromise the standards,
don't compromise your will.
ensure your leadership encourages
your soldiers to charge that hill.

show a little concern,
show a little empathy.
as a leader it's your job to advocate for soldiers,
but that's different from overusing sympathy.

understand your position
and know you don't know it all.
because bad leaders have no influence
and are bound to take a fall.

officer candidate school
is a condensed version of life.
characteristics of a leader vary,
but bad leaders live in strife.

i aim to be the leader i want,
and lead soldiers to success.
because in the army we win,
and we're nothing less than the best.

nature

night gazer

as i stare at the sky in the cold,
brisk night,
i find myself in awe
at such a beautiful sight.

in the bluish, black background,
i can see several constellations;
the magic the experience brings,
is like an inner celebration.

one twinkle of a star,
sets the night sky ablaze;
and i can't look away,
so permanent is my gaze.

never once did i believe i'd be so moved
by this experience;
but i now see how something so random
brings emotional deliverance.

for those who aren't here to see,
it's an incredible travesty.
because the night sky's beauty,
is truly the world's majesty.

the beauty of sight

the world around me so astonishing
and full of opulence.
a speck in a world that has allowed me to see it's
ever changing seasons, and remain an observant occupant.

visions of forestry and cotton ball clouds
a privilege to see.
i watch all the leaves fall,
each one like a rainbow descending from a tree.

a flock of birds gliding by
in a perfect formation.
shiny, patterned shells atop tiny critters;
armoring the seas' crustaceans.

the sun sets in the east,
highlighting the skyline in the distance.
i take in all the beauty of the world,
it's often worth the reminiscence.

emotions & sentimentals

missouri blues

as i sit in this chair, facing the missouri sky;
i relish in my thoughts, analyzing my why.

i'm filled with good energy and positive intuition,
about the future ahead and tackling my ambitions.

somehow my vision is clear, vibrant, full of clarity.
i see greatness in my future, nothing but prosperity.

i know i must live, because one day we take the final fall.
and i would hate to look back, and feel i didn't give my all.

to myself i'm writing this, but my future child will read it.
and i pray that he or she, will take heed and believe it.

maternal

motherhood is so beautiful, seems like a true blessing.
i almost made it that far, but had to learn some life lessons.

i pray the father of my child is a man of good deeds.
i hope to call him husband first, cohesions' what a child needs.

age plays a small factor, but as long as you're healthy;
the time you spend with your kids, the definition of wealthy.

time creeps up on you fast, and brings some troubling thoughts.
but life happens how it should, that's what my elders have taught.

just remember you did the deed, to bring a child in this world.
so be excited either way, if it's a boy or a girl.

i plan to be a great person, and put my character first.
because a mother is what i'll be, when i give my first birth.

a sibling's oath

i am my brother's keeper.
from infancy to adulthood, i've watched you grow and be.
seven years ahead of you, and we rarely disagree.
i'm upset with myself because upon your arrival
i was an envious wreck.
an only child with a new addition on the way,
i didn't know what to expect.

i am my brother's protector.
although i was mean to you,
that was my right as your big sister.
nobody should ever try to emulate that behavior,
unless they desire to be beaten while uttering faint whispers.
i was an emotional hailstorm during adolescence, but i always
wanted to be the best example for my young protégé.
a reflection of me, as a teen i should have listened more
to the unspoken things you had to say.

i am my brother's guardian.
i've made all the mistakes for both you and i.
don't ever let a woman or failure make you cry.
no such thing as a man who can't admit
and apologize when he's wrong.
remember therapy is anything
that brings you peace and comfort,
and it can even be found through song.

i am my brother's confidant.
my best friend in my adult age,
and the only person alive i'd trust with my life's secrets.
and you know if there's a life lesson to be shared,
i'm gonna preach it.

i admire your ability to succeed and overcome
with your male chromosome doner being ever absent.
i abhor his selfish ways that brought sadness to your heart,
in my mind he's already past tense.

i am my brother's support.
as long as i live, you'll always be safe.
even as a grown man, when you call for me,
i'll come running in a cape.
i love you baby bro, and you deserve every verse.
remember to always put your happiness on a pedestal, and put your morals first.

motivational

in professional terms

be professional every time,
it behooves your reputation.
keep that comment to yourself,
and avoid the temptation.

be professional all the time,
there'll be people watching.
have a good work ethic,
be the reason they're talking.

be professional every time,
they're not always right.
but refrain from correcting,
it may take all your might.

be professional all the time,
because your skin is dark.
whether you like it or not,
you must work harder to hit above the mark.

be professional every time,
because success is near.
ignore all the pessimists,
and negativity you hear.

be professional all the time,
always keep your cool.
don't placate to buffoonery,
don't be a belligerent fool.

be professional every time,
because you know that you should.
use common sense and tact,
like you know that you could.

be professional all the time,
it'll make you better.
and you can use that description in your
recommendation letter.

be professional every time,
cause' you're a worthy being.
and watch the pure satisfaction
and accomplishment it brings.

be professional all the time,
and contain that rage.
it will assist you with options,
later in your old age.

be professional every time,
i'm giving you a life lesson.
just remember what i said,
and accept your blessings.

graduation day

i graduated from high school, yea okay it was fun.
i celebrated with a cookout, a few hours out in the sun.

yea i graduated from junior college, now that was a blast;
my education is moving quickly, i do learn pretty fast.

then i graduated from undergrad, as a student-athlete.
the one thing i know quite well, is that i'll always compete.

i got my master's degree complete, as a full-time cop
i can't seem to slow down, it's just not worth it to stop.

next, i became a soldier, graduated from bct.
what's that saying the army has? oh yea, "be all you can be".

okay, i graduated to womanhood, my choices my own.
so much to learn, more so than college, i couldn't do it alone.

before i could promote my mindset, i had to graduate my thoughts.
i need to nurture my growth, it's always tranquility i've sought.

can't wait to see my next graduation, i wonder what'll be.
i'm still laying the foundation; guess i'll just have to wait and see.

fury

i'm better than second best,
no interest in accepting mediocrity;
i'm sorry you think because i'm intense,
i lack generosity.

no passion, no gain,
pains endured by the best.
high stakes, all fury,
be better than the rest.

confidence is built,
it's earned like respect.
only you know your next triumph,
it's the best secret kept.

be aggressive, be explosive,
be driven and succeed.
all gas, no brakes,
the road to winning is high speed.

get amped, look alive,
because this experience is for you.
you get one life, one ride,
there will never be two.

for as long as i live,
the fire within me will never die.
it's the adhesive to my core,
it's what keeps me alive.

inspiration

beautiful inspiration.
you illuminate like sun rays.
i frequently embrace your essence.
although you may not always be near,
i cherish the clarity you bring
when i'm able to feel your energy.
my life hungers for your presence.
i crave you mentally.
you invoke growth, and give me hope.
continue to radiate my path.
you inspire my wrath.

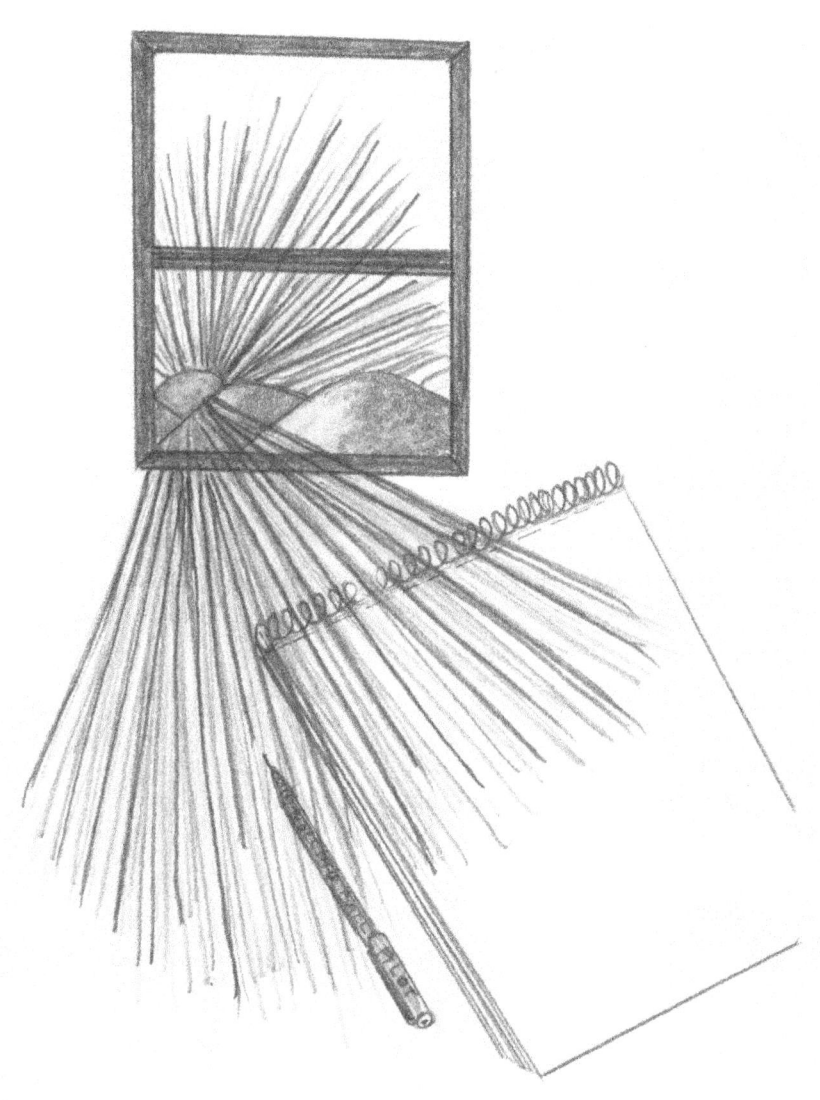

authority

i have the authority to be up in the place.
i know my belonging threw you off, due to my race.

i have the authority to walk the town.
i see you looking, face balled up in a frown.

i have the authority to access new education.
sometimes i have to breath and restore my vivation.

i have the authority to lead the masses.
it's natural born for me, you should stick to the classes.

i have the authority to be who i am.
i possess potential overload, confidence filled to the brim.

i have the authority to speak my mind.
no fear in my heart; fear and victory don't align.

i have the authority just like you.
i rebuke oppressive mindsets, and you should too.

i have the authority to live my life.
live yours too, regret cuts like a knife.

inquisition

what happens when you reach the top,
does it hurt any less?
and was it really worth your time,
do you have your regrets?

what happened to the happy family
that you said you would make?
and will your money and accolades
give to you, or just take?

when did you decide you'd only wear
fancy clothes with a label?
and do you feel alone at home
as you sit at your table?

where are those friends and family
who said they'd be there till' the end?
they seem to only show their face
when you have money to spend.

why did you choose the popular chick
on the cheerleading team?
the studious girl with the future
should have been first it seems.

what happens years later
as you slow down and digress?
will you have lived a full life,
or just have lived for success?

i know we hustle hard to be
and leave our societal mark.
just find the balance that you need;
remember success is an art.

mental health & mindfulness

an idle mind's despair
*For O. Martinez, emotions are what make us human;
control and perspective is what make things tolerable.*

don't let your psyche fall
and make reality a blur.
don't do something you'll regret,
and let a suicide occur.

don't be the reason for that silence
when your family mourns;
you are the reason they made that bond,
since the day you were born.
don't let that falling sensation be your main condition, restore;
don't leave your parents with sorrow, regret,
and all the questions galore.

despair won't last forever,
look up to the sky and believe.
just know that anything you do
you must execute to conceive.

you have to exercise your will to live
to make your life great,
or choose to take away from others,
and create unbearable weight.

don't think a disappearance from this world
will make it much better;
the only trace of your remembrance
will be through a letter.

just hold on breath and think,
and let the despair subside.
cause only growth and pain add worth to the experience,
standfast for the ride.

a reflective freefall

i'm my own worst enemy,
this i must admit.
i tend to go all out;
i tend to over commit.

it's a reputable trait,
but it can come at a cost.
my personal life pays the price,
it usually takes the loss.

i'd rather be the leader
and be the one for decisions.
i'm ready for the backlash and critiques
pointed with precision.

i've always been motivated,
i never had to be told;
way too competitive for that,
too bold to ever fold.

i think about me a lot,
how i've changed over the years.
i've taken some beneficial risks;
i even left a career.

i had it all planned out,
i had it written in stone.
but things changed up a bit,
i'm really setting the tone.

death really changed my perspective,
cause when my grandfather died;
i remembered failure and fear,
they can both be defied.

i've seen that envy is real,
people will smile in your face.
and pray hard for your downfall,
and be ready to fill in your place.

not sure why the world is so cold,
i guess it has to be.
it's the only way through,
the only time to be free.

i want my words to be heard.
i want the people to see.
a piece of my creative side,
and what it's like to be me.

i'm tough, quiet, emotional,
and i desire a bond.
you can tell in my writing,
that i want love to be fond.

of me, we, and he,
and we can figure it out.
cause' happiness is my ultimate journey;
lord, please provide me the route.

uncategorical

directionless

floating through life with no aim,
without a care.
sometimes good things come to those who wait;
sometimes it doesn't, it seems unfair.

rolling through life,
unwilling to settle for one thing.
eliminating my hunger for passions
because a living is necessary, and cash is king.

strolling through life,
daydreaming as the world turns.
unbothered by judgment,
except from those who matter; then it burns.

walking through life,
the physical aging as i do.
my travels through this life
is understood by a many few.

be realistic

be realistic and continue to believe in those dreams of yours.
there is nothing more valuable
than having a vision and wearing and wanting more.

be realistic and aspire for whatever you please.
my dream is to travel and write,
while being afloat beautiful, exotic seas.

be realistic, go pursue and live your desires.
i'll continue to live a life of meaning
with an unextinguishable fire.

be realistic and show the world the beauty within you.
it's difficult sometimes, but even the sky
goes through changes; it's not always blue.

be realistic and become who you are supposed to be.
i've chosen to live my life fearless, empowered,
and enthusiastically.

unsettled

i will never settle again.

that's meant for people, lost opportunities, and sunken places. my existence has evolved; i've seen the world and several faces.
my family and sanity mean the world to me.
i find the path that's right and let it be.

i will never settle again.

i've been called everything but a child of god.
i believe in that saying, spoil the child because of a spared rod.
i believe the rod should be mostly metaphorical;
why tarnish your creation, and risk a punishment that's categorical.

i will never settle again.

my life has been a true blessin'.
i've decided to live it to the fullest with minimal stressin'.
i swear by anita baker and marvin gaye.
they put me in my zone, no matter the time of day.

i will never settle again.

i made plans that didn't come to pass.
i had the right idea but moved a little bit too fast.
i live in color and like to take my pictures with the flash.
i store all the bad times and failures in my memory's trash.

i will never settle again.

i consider myself a literal gem.
a diamond in the rough, exuberance from every limb.
i want to activate your new ideas and thoughts.
my attention and loyalty is something that's granted, not bought.

i will never settle again.

i'm old enough to understand emotion.
i hate exaggerated people who cause unnecessary commotion.
give me positivity and peace in my journey.
i'd rather talk it out with people, and not an attorney.

i will never settle again.

the color black

the color black is so versatile
and coordinates well.
so why is it when it's attached
to a group, it doesn't sell?

the color black has so many shades
and varying complexions.
i'm this way every day; no life filters,
no changes, no exceptions.

the color black is associated with evil, darkness, despair,
and the time of day that is night.
but without it, how would you ever know the feeling
of overcoming and seeing the light?

the color black is the definition of creating
a true fighting chance.
the beauty of blackness is real,
you could never change my stance.

90's baby

crazy, sexy, cool like tlc.
nobody had better music than 90's rnb.
denzel, eddie, & angela took over the movie screens;
a smooth, sexy, historic moment in every scene.

nickelodeon used to be so intellectual and real;
i was never really a disney kid,
but they had a few shows that had some appeal.
baggy clothes, starter jackets, and afros freshly sheened.
everybody had a pair of nike, reebok, or pumas
they rocked with their respective jeans.

those apartment kids were so creative
and knew how to have fun.
we double-dutched, jumped out of swings, traded insults,
and raced until we could no longer run.
the candy lady knew us all by name.
we would even take a walk down to her house
in the pouring rain.

i saw the delinquency in a few of my peers, even through play.
unfortunately they grew older and fit the description,
and i mentioned to others, "i saw it back in the day".
the 90s felt like home, and oh how i miss those days.
that was the first time i was introduced to alvin ailey,
and got a chance to see a live play.

take me back to the good ol' days, is truly an understatement.
i'm here letting 90s flavor live on;
i could never let it remain latent.
i miss the authenticity of all those nostalgic vibes.
everybody felt like family, and we were truly on a quest
to become a familial tribe.

colors
For M. Bennett, a kind soul. Thank you for allowing me to be inclusive in my writing.

i had a peer ask me
to write about lgbt.
at first, i hesitated
because it doesn't relate to me.

but then i realized progressive minds
should respect others first.
even if you disagree and
think it's something not on your turf.

some of the most talented people
identify with lgbtq.
how would it feel if you were involved,
and others outcasted you?

do you have strength to go all out
and live a life in your truth?
cause we grow older and forget
the free will we had in our youth.

i can't say that i was totally comfortable,
but i wanted to accommodate a friend;
and who am i to judge,
no one living is bigger than sin.

whatever genre of sexuality
makes you feel great.
you must accept your reality,
and ignore all the hate.

i wholeheartedly support
your decision to live as you are.
that confidence in life will surely
help you maintain and go far.

as quiet as it's kept

i know he's a liar,
but he's physically appealing.
my spirit detects dishonesty,
but my senses are repealing.
a smooth talker, a quick tongue,
and charisma to match.
he didn't have to work hard to be seen,
or for my attention to catch.

sin comes in all shapes,
shades, and dimensions;
i'm falling in, deep,
against my own contention.
a stare so direct,
i'm instantly informed.
whether right or wrong,
my mind has already conformed.

a question asked,
and i know he's every bit of deceptive.
my body's being forgiving,
and ready to be receptive.
a forever mystery and
a guest for the night.
i'm a mystery myself,
and entertaining him in spite.

never be the pot calling the kettle black,
it's beyond hypocritical;
even though i've dawned my vengeance,
i'll be nothing but hospitable.
i'm off the path that crossed us into passion,
and my how the tables have turned.
i'm suddenly bombarded with apologies and pleads,
as if he's a lover scorned.

i thought the game was for everybody;
time to go back to the drawing board?
too late, new management in place,
and i've already scored.
next time come prepared
for the unexpected, it comes in handy.
remember this experience,
play fair, and things will be just dandy.

an ode to jill*

i'm living my life
like it's golden;
my pride and joy in tact,
it could never be stolen.

a long walk away from the end,
and i'm here for it all.
a true virgo, and the essence of me
is similar to the mystic beauty of fall.

let me show you the way to my mind's core,
and my most intimate depths.
i welcome you to my life,
but my heart is the only source that denies or accepts.

hesitancy and stubbornness seem to be
gettin' in the way of me and you.
i want your love and focus,
not money and gifts in lieu.

he loves me, he loves me not,
is something for kids; it's simply child's play.
i'm one to watch your actions, listening closely
to your exact words to hear exactly what you say.

so gone in the present,
mastering my ability to become one from within.
i am truly the master of my fate,
nobody else; this i will contend.

---

*   An Ode to Jill is a poem incorporating the titles of a few of Jill Scott's songs. I am a fan of her music style.

support that business

support that business,
and stop tryna' get stuff for free.
that person bought my entire collection,
and looks nothing like me.

support that business,
because why not support a friend?
bring their vision to life,
spend a few dividends.

support that business because
you know it's of quality.
you get the truth in every verse,
no fillers or apologies.

support that business because
it's one of a kind.
don't be envious of a good thing,
just let it shine.

support that business because
you would want others to do it for you.
i could use your hand in my success,
but believe and know that i will always see it through.

hormonal oblivion

i met someone new,
i'm having a hormonal fight.
i feel he's no good,
i know something ain't right.

he looks good for a short while,
he's attractive by all means.
he'll humor you for a while,
but in your future there's no ring.

i'm bored with the single life
and physicality interests most.
i may feel a spark in the moment,
but the truth is we'll never be close.

he's filled with lustful liquids
and his cup runneth over.
danger in the flesh,
i abstain holding a 4-leafed clover.

bring me luck cause' i'm weak
and a little jaded.
i have a short-term interest,
and after conversation that has faded.

tonight, i choose pleasure,
give me all the best.
i met him on a saturday,
but on the lord's day i rest.

perspective

i stepped in a pile shit, and yes it did smear.
but on the flip side of that, i still have my career.

i saw a woman get slapped and that just ain't right.
but on the flip side of that, i still have my sight.

i fell on the concrete hard and scraped up my knee.
but on the flip side of that, i still have the ability to be.

i'm a perfectionist individual and sometimes i raise hell.
but on the flip side of that, my ambition refuses to fail.

www.ingramcontent.com/pod-product-compliance
Lightning Source LLC
Chambersburg PA
CBHW060851050426
42453CB00008B/931